A Children's Christmas Musical
Teaching the Blessing of Giving

Created by Pam Andrews

Arranged by John DeVries

LILLENAS
PUBLISHING COMPANY

lillenas.com

Contents

CHARACTERS

Cast

Mrs. Sanders

Clara Sanders

Levi Sanders

Mr. Goodman

Tommy

Toys

GI Jeff

Baby Doll

Hatchbox Car

Shine Bear

Shepherd Boy

Actors

Joseph

Mary

Several needy families

Joyland Overture

includes

Shine Your Light for Jesus
God's Got a Plan for Me

Arr. by John DeVries

*"God's Got a Plan for You"

Joyland Christmas

with

Joy to the World

Words and Music by
PAM ANDREWS
Arr. by John DeVries

10

2nd time to Coda ⊕
(to pg. 12, meas. 32)

D.S. al Coda
(to pg. 10, meas. 13)

Glo - ry, hal - le - lu - jah, glo - ry to our King!

CODA

Je - sus, we a - dore You,

Sav - ior and our King; Je - sus, we a -

dore You, our all, our ev - 'ry - thing; You

14

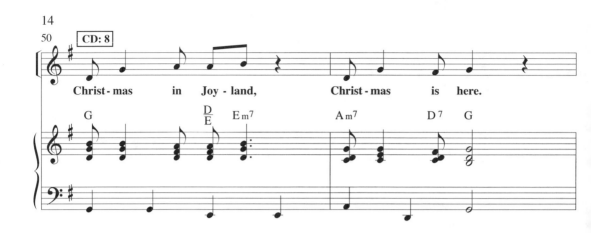

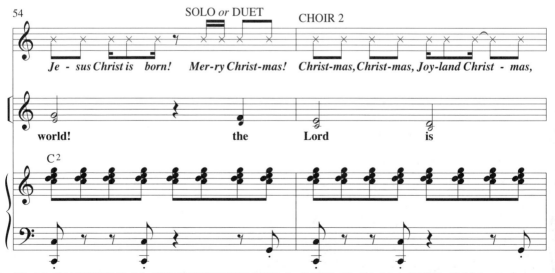

*Words by ISAAC WATTS; Music by GEORGE FREDERICK HANDEL. Arr. © 2006 by Pilot Point Music (ASCAP). All rights reserved.
Administered by The Copyright Company, 1025 16th Avenue South, Suite 204, Nashville, TN 37212.

Scene 1

(MRS. SANDERS enters the Joyland Toy Store with her two children, CLARA and LEVI. MR. GOODMAN is behind the check-out counter. TOMMY, store helper, is busy sweeping the floor.)

MRS. SANDERS: Come along, children, we only have a few minutes. We just need to buy a gift for the church Toy Store.

(MR. GOODMAN, dusting, overhears the conversation between children and MRS. SANDERS.)

MR. GOODMAN: What can I do for you on this Christmas Eve, Mrs. Sanders? Getting in some last minute shopping?

MRS. SANDERS: I guess you could say that. The kids and I are buying a gift for the Christmas Toy Store at church. We want to drop it off on the way home. We're just trying to find something that will meet our budget. Things have been a little tight this year. *(looks longingly at the toys)*

MR. GOODMAN: Why don't you pass on the toy store gift and just take care of your own two children?

MRS. SANDERS: Oh, no. Giving to the church Toy Store at Christmas has been a family tradition for years. David and I always wanted the kids to know it is more blessed to give than to receive. Children, see if you can find something, not too expensive.

CLARA: Sure thing, Mom. Levi, look at all the toys. I love that pretty Baby Doll and that Shine Bear. *(looks at SHINE BEAR)* Oh, no, it's light must be broken.

LEVI: Hey, that Hatchbox Car is awesome! And look, there's a GI Jeff. *(to Mom)* What about this toy? *(holds up a giant stuffed animal)*

CLARA: Yes, mom, this would be great!

MRS. SANDERS: I don't know kids. That toy looks kind of expensive. Maybe you should look for something else.

MR. GOODMAN: Why kids, that's a great choice. That toy has been on the shelf for some time, so it has a clearance price, $2.98.

MRS. SANDERS *(relieved)*: $2.98? Are you sure, Mr. Goodman?

MR. GOODMAN: Quite sure.

MRS. SANDERS: Perfect, Thank you, Mr. Goodman.

(MR. GOODMAN and MRS. SANDERS move to the checkout counter)

MRS. SANDERS: Let me see. I'm sure I have $2.98. *(looks for money in the bottom of her purse)* Here's a dollar. Now, let's see if I can find the change.

MR. GOODMAN: That's alright, Mrs. Sanders. I can cover the rest.

MRS. SANDERS: No, here, I have it.

(She hands Mr. Goodman the money. He puts the money in the cash register and gives her a receipt.)

MRS. SANDERS: Come along children. It's time to go.

(LEVI and CLARA run to MRS. SANDERS. They move toward the door.)

CLARA: Mom, can we carry the toy to the car?

MRS. SANDERS: It's "may we," and yes, you may.

LEVI: Okay, mom. C'mon, Clara.

MR. GOODMAN: Good night, Mrs. Sanders. Merry Christmas!

TOMMY: Good night, ma'am. We'll be open bright and early on the 26th for the "After Christmas Sale."

Mrs. Sanders: Goodnight and Merry Christmas.

(Mrs. Sanders, Levi, and Clara exit SR.)

Tommy: Finally, the last customer out the door!

Mr. Goodman (stares out the door after looking at Mrs. Sanders): What a long day! It seems like December 24th is getting busier every year. My feet are aching. Tommy, how about you do one quick dusting of those leftover toys?

(Mr. Goodman hands Tommy the feather duster)

Tommy: Sure thing, Mr. Goodman.

(Tommy places the broom in the corner and takes the feather duster from Mr. Goodman. He begins to dust the toys.)

Tommy: Don't you think it's kind of a shame?

Mr. Goodman: What's that, Tommy?

Tommy: It seems kind of sad these toys are left.

Mr. Goodman: I know what you mean, but they'll be sold in our big after Christmas sale.

Tommy: Yes, sir. I know. It's just a shame they'll not be under someone's Christmas tree this year. By the way, did anyone ever call you about this shepherd? (holds up the shepherd)

Mr. Goodman: No, I guess the people who bought that nativity scene never missed him.

Tommy: Too bad. (finishes dusting the toys) That about does it, Mr. Goodman. If it's okay with you, I think I'll be heading out. My mom wants me home as early as possible. Should I turn off the manger scene lights in front of the store?

Mr. Goodman: No. Leave' em be, Tommy. That manger scene reminds us all that Christmas is Jesus' birthday. I'm heading to church. There's a special Christmas Eve meeting tonight, something about some needy families and the Christmas Toy Store. Can I give you a ride?

Tommy: No, thanks, Mr. Goodman. My mom's picking me up.

MR. GOODMAN: Oh, my! *(checks his watch)* Look at the time! I'm supposed to be at church in 15 minutes. Let's go. I'll see you the day after Christmas…bright and early.

TOMMY: 8:00 a.m. sharp. Good night, Mr. Goodman.

MR. GOODMAN: Good night, Tommy.

(They both exit the scene. TOMMY exits stage right and MR. GOODMAN stage left. The toy wake-up music is played. The smoke appears and disguises toy actors entering quickly stage right and left to replace the toys. They should just place the pretend toys behind the shelf and take their place. The SHEPHERD BOY also joins the toys on the shelf.)

Toy Wake-up Music

Music and Arr. by
JOHN DEVRIES

GI JEFF *(GI voice; suddenly the toys come to life.)*: Attention!

(toys pop to attention)

GI JEFF: At ease, everyone.

(toys relax)

HATCHBOX CAR: I thought they would never leave. Achoooo! *(blows his nose)*

SHINE BEAR: God bless you, Hatchbox Car.

HATCHBOX CAR: If that kid doesn't stop dusting us with that feather monster, I think I'm gonna scream!

SHINE BEAR: Come on Hatchbox, Tommy's nice…so's Mr. Goodman. You're just in a bad mood.

GI JEFF: Affirmative. Aren't we all? Just look at us…the leftovers. The toys nobody wants.

HATCHBOX CAR: Right, GI Jeff. I had such dreams for this year. Racing around the track in some kid's room on Christmas Day *(pretends to drive around the room)*…but, here I am…parked on the sideline…a toy reject.

BABY DOLL *(crying)*: Waaaaaaa! I want my mommy!!!

SHINE BEAR: Calm down, Baby Doll. Everything's gonna be alright.

(SHINE BEAR pats BABY DOLL)

HATCHBOX CAR: Can I get you some water, Baby Doll? Would that make you feel better?

(HATCHBOX CAR offers BABY DOLL a glass of water)

SHINE BEAR: Don't you know that you should NEVER give a Baby Doll water? That could be a disaster!

BABY DOLL *(crying)*: Light up, Shine Bear. That always makes me feel better.

SHINE BEAR: I can't Baby Doll. A kid was looking at me the other day and dropped me on the floor. My batteries fell out and rolled away.

BABY DOLL: How terrible. Waaaaaa! *(crying)*

HATCHBOX CAR: Shift down, Baby Doll. Put it in cruise control.

BABY DOLL *(whining)*: I wanted to be under a Christmas tree this year. Why do I have to be a baby doll? Why couldn't I have been one of those cool dolls with all the accessories? Baby dolls aren't "in" anymore.

GI JEFF: Soldiers, get a grip. Remember, Christmas is happening at 6 hundred hours. There's still time for a miracle. It's happened before!

SHINE BEAR: You're right, GI Jeff. Come on, everyone. Let's get some Christmas cheer happening! Even if we are leftover toys, we can still be happy on Christmas.

(music begins)

Let Us Bring Joy to You

Words and Music by
PAM ANDREWS
Arr. by John DeVries

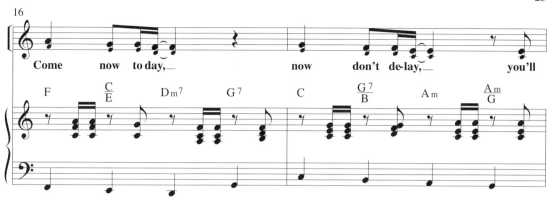

Come now to day,— now don't de-lay,— you'll

F | C/E | Dm7 | G7 | C | G7/B | Am | Am/G

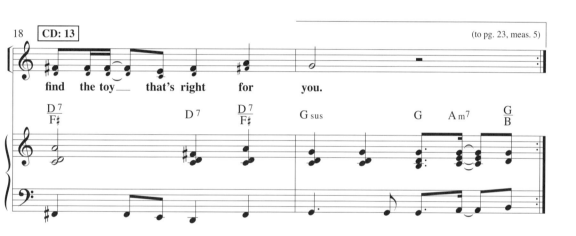

find the toy— that's right for you.

(to pg. 23, meas. 5)

CD: 13

D7/F♯ | D7 | D7/F♯ | G sus | G | Am7 | G/B

1st time: GI JEFF
2nd time: BABY DOLL
mf

I am strong and I am rough;
Ba - by dolls are here to stay;

F | C | G | C | C (no 3)

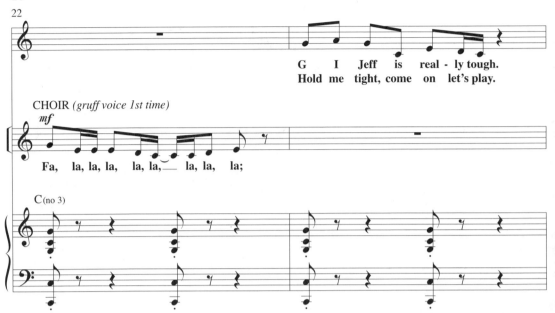

G I Jeff is real - ly tough.
Hold me tight, come on let's play.

CHOIR (gruff voice 1st time)

Fa, la, la, la, la, la, la, la, la;

C(no 3)

Fa, la, la, la, la, la,

Fa, la, la, la, la, la, la, la, la,

C(no 3)   G(no 3)   C(no 3)

1st time: HATCHBOX
2nd time: SHINE BEAR

I'm a crus-in' toy ma-chine;
Bears bring joy to ev-'ry-thing;

Fa, la, la, la, la, la.

Cut-ting curves, I'm real-ly mean.
With bat-ter-ies a light I'll bring.

CHOIR
Fa, la, la, la, la, la, la, la, la;

30

Fa, la, la, la, la, la, Fa, la, la, la, la, la, — la, la, la,

C(no 3)   G(no 3)   C(no 3)

32

Fa, la, la, la, la, la. Joy - land, joy - land,

C(no 3)   G(no 3)   C(no 3)   F   Em7

CD: 15 *1st time*

CD: 16 *2nd time*

34

what an awe - some place, Joy - land, joy - land with

Dm7   G9   C   C7   F   Em7

36

| 1 | (to pg. 25, meas. 21) ‖ | 2 |

smiles on ev - 'ry face! smiles on ev - 'ry face!

D7sus   D7 G7   D7sus   D7 G7

Scene 2

SHEPHERD BOY (*joins the other toys center stage*): That was awesome, you guys.

GI JEFF: Affirmative, son. Who are you?

SHEPHERD BOY: I'm the Shepherd Boy from the $14.95 nativity set…you know, the one that was in the window all month.

GI JEFF: Where's the rest of your platoon, soldier?

HATCHBOX CAR: Didn't you hear? A family saw the nativity display in the store window…

SHINE BEAR: And as Mr. Goodman was showing them the box, the Shepherd fell on the floor.

BABY DOLL: He tried the best that any toy can try to be noticed…

HATCHBOX CAR: But Mr. Goodman put the box in a bag leaving the Shepherd on the floor. The family left…never to return.

BABY DOLL: How terrible! I think I might cry. Waaaaaa!

(SHINE BEAR *covers her mouth.*)

SHINE BEAR: Enough already, Baby Doll.

HATCHBOX CAR: Right, the kid feels bad enough as it is.

(SHEPHERD BOY *moves to stage left and stands as if waiting.*)

BABY DOLL: After Christmas, he'll probably end up in that scary blue thing behind the store…the "dumpster." Waa….

(GI JEFF *holds up his hand and stops her mid-cry.*)

GI JEFF *(interrupting)*: Excuse, me, Shepherd Boy. *(moves to the* SHEPHERD BOY*)* What are you doing?

SHEPHERD BOY: Waiting for my ride, sir. I just know my owner will come to take me home soon.

(Toys gather around the SHEPHERD BOY.*)*

HATCHBOX CAR: Get real, kid. No one's coming for you. You're a leftover. There'll be no car ride for you today.

GI JEFF: Pipe down, Hatchbox Car. *(to the* SHEPHERD BOY*)* I'm sorry, son, but he is correct. The platoon and I are here for you if there is anything we can do.

SHEPHERD BOY: Thank you, but I'm fine. There's a home out there waiting for me. God's got a plan for this small Shepherd Boy! I just know it!

(Music begins; during the song, the SHEPHERD BOY *moves across the stage. He ends the song center stage.)*

God's Got a Plan for Me

Words and Music by
PAM ANDREWS
Arr. by John DeVries

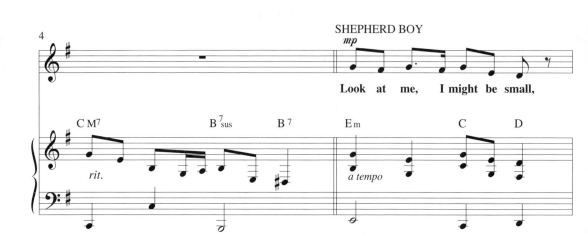

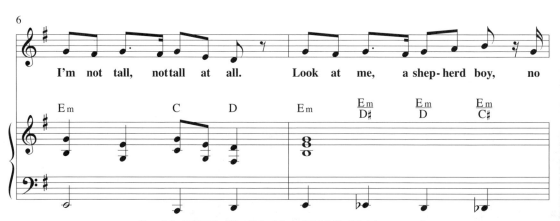

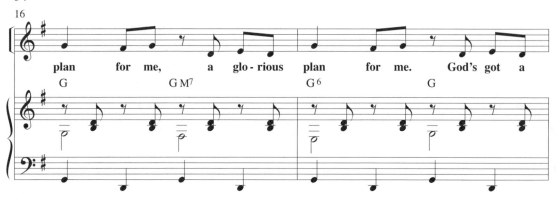

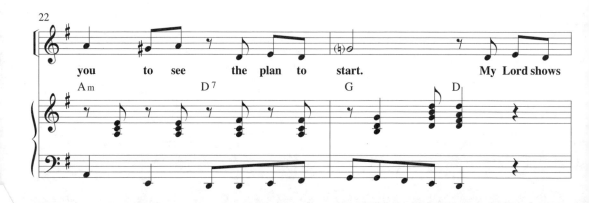

SHEPHERD BOY

32

Gon - na come and save me from this lone - ly life.

Gon - na send me peace and joy and His Christ-mas light.

CD: 20

Gon - na help me, gon - na love me, Gon - na show the way.

Gon - na be my friend for - ev - er, that's His plan to - day.

Slower ♩ = ca. 96   CHOIR and SOLO

God's got a plan for me, a glo-rious plan for me. God's got a plan for me, He knows my heart. God's got a plan for me, yes sir, a plan in-deed. Can't wait for

accel. poco a poco

Joyful, faster ♩ = ca. 118

38

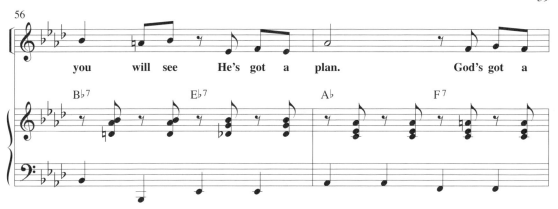

you will see He's got a plan. God's got a

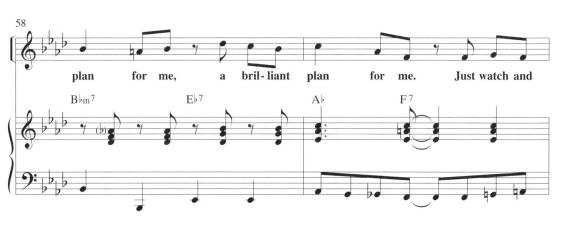

plan for me, a bril- liant plan for me. Just watch and

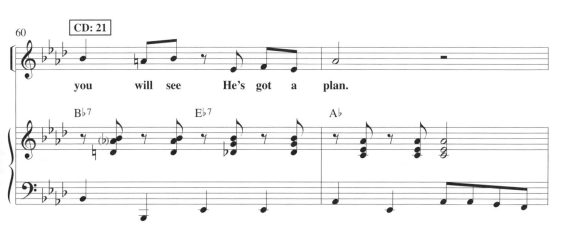

you will see He's got a plan.

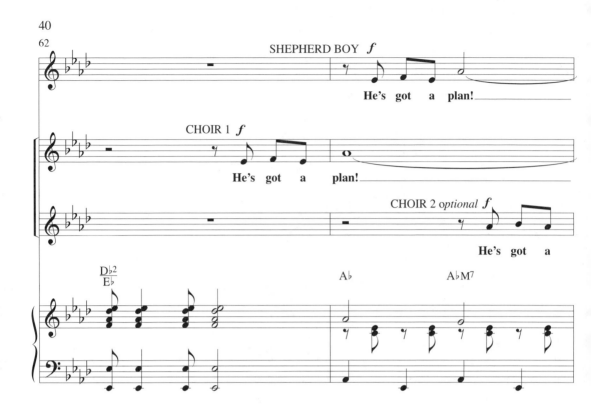

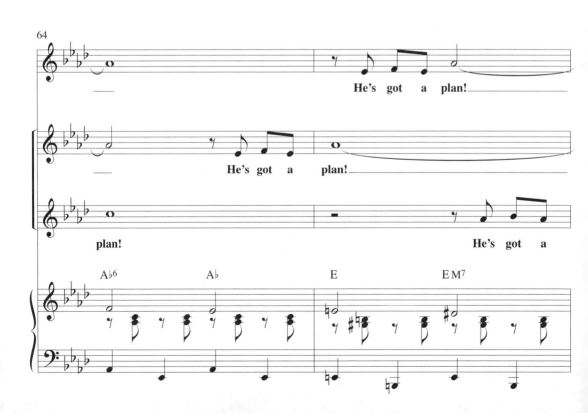

Scene 3

(Toys move center stage to join the Shepherd Boy.*)*

GI Jeff: That bump on your head has you off target, son.

Baby Doll: Just thinking about your fall makes me…dizzy. *(acts like she could faint)*

HATCHBOX CAR *(to* SHEPHERD BOY*)*: Gear down to reality kid. You're racing down the wrong road.

GI JEFF: I'll give it to you straight, soldier. You're alone. *(points to himself)* You're just like the rest of us…leftovers.

BABY DOLL: Waaaaaaaaaa!

SHEPHERD BOY: God will get me to my family. I know it. And He'll get you to yours.

GI JEFF: I hope you're right…but your chances look negative. Let's make the best of our situation and get focused. Stand up straight. Don't slouch! We want to look sharp for the After Christmas Sale.

SHINE BEAR: I could stand up as straight as an arrow, but no one would want me. Who wants a Shine Bear with no shine?

SHEPHERD BOY *(to* SHINE BEAR*)*: God has a plan for you, Shine Bear. He wants you to shine a smile on some kid's face. Come on, everyone, let's look for those batteries.

HATCHBOX CAR: I'm with you, Shepherd Boy.

SHINE BEAR: Thanks, everyone. I really appreciate it.

BABY DOLL: Waaaaaaaa! *(crying)*

HATCHBOX CAR: Why are you crying now, Baby Doll?

BABY DOLL: I don't know where to look.

SHEPHERD BOY: You're the smallest, so you look under the counter.

GI JEFF: Commence Operation Battery Recon. Here's the mission…Fan out, soldiers, and find those batteries. Move it, move it, move it!

(All the toys begin to look for the batteries. They look quietly as the scene shifts to stage right and the family scene. MRS. SANDERS, LEVI and CLARA enter the family living room scene from stage left. They are obviously a poor family. There is a small Christmas tree with few or no presents.)

MRS. SANDERS: Clara and Levi Sanders! It's bedtime, kids!

LEVI: I can't wait to go to bed, mom, because when I wake up it'll be Christmas.

CLARA: Me, too. I hope I get a pretty baby doll for Christmas or a Shine Bear like we saw at the store.

LEVI: No girly stuff for me…send me one of those GI men or a cool car.

MRS. SANDERS *(looking sad)*: Children, this year, Christmas will be a little different. You know it's been hard for me to even buy food and pay our bills. So, as for Christmas and lots of presents…

LEVI *(interrupting)*: That's okay, mom. We understand.

CLARA: Yeah. Don't worry about it, mom. We're just happy we're together.

LEVI: I sure miss Dad.

CLARA: Me, too. Do you think he's celebrating Christmas in heaven, mom?

MRS. SANDERS: I know he is. This Christmas dad will be with Jesus, but we'll be together. We might not have as many gifts, but we will still have Christmas Joy.

LEVI: You will still read us the Christmas story, won't you, mom?

CLARA: And we can still sing our Christmas carols?

MRS. SANDERS: Of course, why don't we sing dad's favorite right now?

(music begins)

What Child Is This?

with
Jesus Baby

WILLIAM C. DIX

Traditional English Melody
Arr. by John DeVries

Hal - le - lu - jah   in the high - est,   King of kings___ is

born   to - day.   Hal - le - lu - jah,   God Al-might - y,

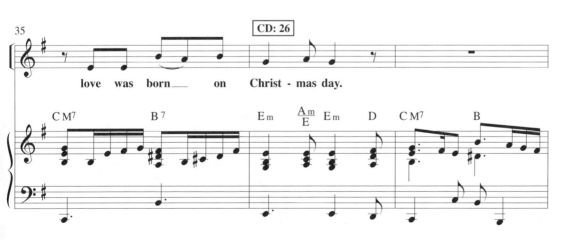

love was born___ on Christ - mas day.

CD: 26

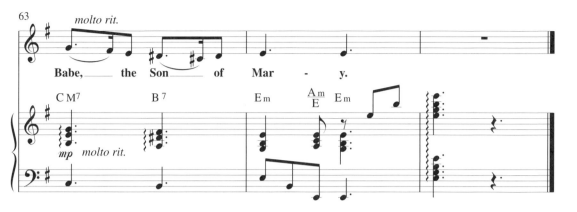

Scene 4

MRS. SANDERS: Oh, yes, kids! I do have a surprise for you. I found this Nativity Set tossed in the trash at work. It's only missing a Shepherd. You can put it under the tree.

(Kids place the nativity under the tree.)

CLARA: It looks great!

LEVI *(disappointed)*: Sure wish we had the Shepherd, though.

CLARA: I'm sure that Shepherd is feeling lost and alone. He must be missing his family.

MRS. SANDERS: Think of it this way, maybe he's out looking for lost sheep and he'll be back when he's found them.

CLARA: I like that.

LEVI: Me, too.

MRS. SANDERS *(hugs the kids)*: Everything's going to be okay, kids. I just wish we could afford a turkey. Christmas just won't be the same without giving each of you a drumstick. Oh well, never mind. It's time you guys say your prayers and hop in bed. Levi, it's your turn to pray.

LEVI: Okay. *(kneels)* Dear God, Merry Christmas. We hope you're having a great birthday party in heaven with a big cake and lots of balloons. Tell my dad hello and that I love him and I really miss him. Help mom not to worry about Christmas this year. We know times are rough. Lord, if you could help do one thing…get mom a turkey…She really loves cooking turkey and we love those drumsticks. Thanks, Lord. Amen. Goodnight, mom. Merry Christmas!

CLARA: Goodnight, mom!

MRS. SANDERS: Thanks for understanding about Christmas. Things will get better. Now off to bed!

(LEVI, CLARA, and MRS. SANDERS exit stage right. The focus shifts back to the toy store scene.)

BABY DOLL *(finds batteries under the counter)*: I found 'em! I found 'em!

(SHINE BEAR runs to BABY DOLL at the counter. BABY DOLL is holding up the batteries.)

SHINE BEAR: My batteries! My precious batteries! Oh, thank you, Baby Doll. Could you please put them in?

BABY DOLL: Me? I would love to, darling. *(pretends to put the batteries in the back of SHINE BEAR and turns on the lights)*

HATCHBOX CAR: Look at Shine Bear!

GI JEFF: Mission accomplished!

SHINE BEAR: I'm all better! I can shine! I can shine!

(music begins)

Shine Your Light for Jesus

Words and Music by
PAM ANDREWS
Arr. by John DeVries

Shine your light for Je - sus, let it

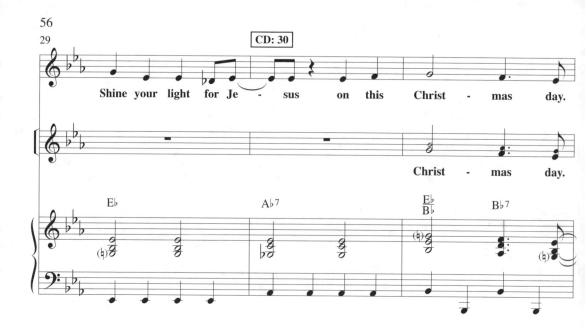

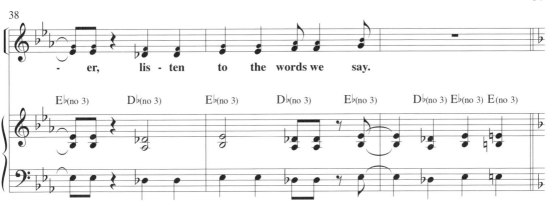

er, lis - ten to the words we say.

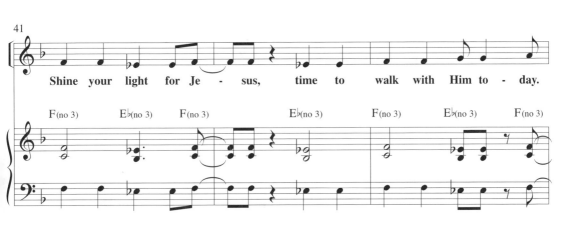

Shine your light for Je - sus, time to walk with Him to - day.

CD: 31

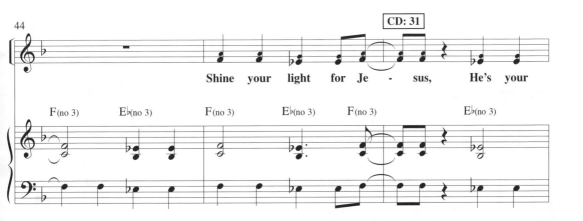

Shine your light for Je - sus, He's your

59

64

Scene 5

GI JEFF: Get some shuteye, soldiers. We want to look our best for the After Christmas Sale.

SHINE BEAR: Maybe the Shepherd Boy is right. There <u>is</u> someone out there waiting for us.

(All the toys settle down to sleep except the SHEPHERD BOY *and* SHINE BEAR.*)*

TOYS: Goodnight! See you in the morning! Night everyone!

GI JEFF: Lights out!

(The SHEPHERD BOY *walks stage left and sits on the corner of the stage as if waiting for his family.* SHINE BEAR *comes and sits by him.)*

SHINE BEAR: Shepherd Boy, why aren't you going to sleep? You know GI Jeff sent us to bed.

SHEPHERD BOY: I guess I'm a little homesick for the rest of my family. I know they're out there waiting for me.

SHINE BEAR: Try to get some sleep. Things will look better in the morning. It will be Christmas!

SHEPHERD BOY: Thanks, Shine Bear. I will. *(sits down on the floor stage left)*

*(*LEVI *enters from stage right and* CLARA *follows closely behind.)*

CLARA *(taps* LEVI *on the shoulder)*: Levi, Mom, told us to go to bed.

LEVI: I will in a minute, Clara. There's just one more thing I need to do. You go ahead. I'll be there in a minute.

CLARA: Okay, see you in the morning.

LEVI *(kneels)*: Lord, I forgot something. If you see that missing Shepherd somewhere, could you send it my way? He must miss his family, and I know what it's like to miss someone. Thank You, Jesus. I know You're out there. I know You'll take care of us. I love you. Amen.

(Music begins; LEVI *stands stage right to sing the song with the* SHEPHERD BOY *who stands stage left.)*

I Know You're Out There

Words and Music by
PAM ANDREWS
Arr. by John DeVries

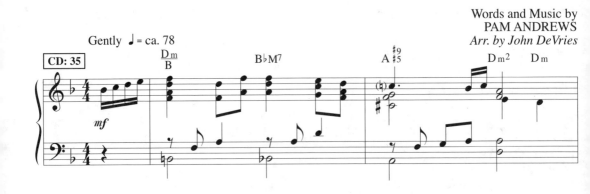

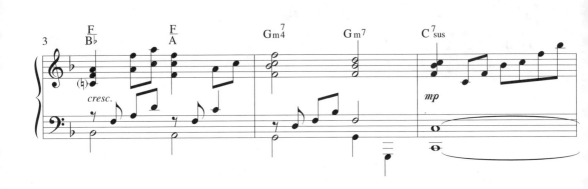

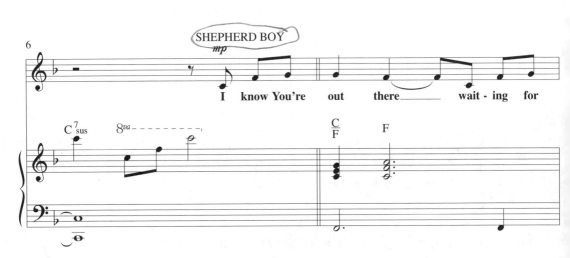

SHEPHERD BOY

I know You're out there_____ wait-ing for

70

72

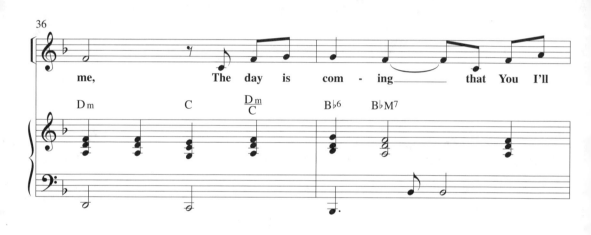

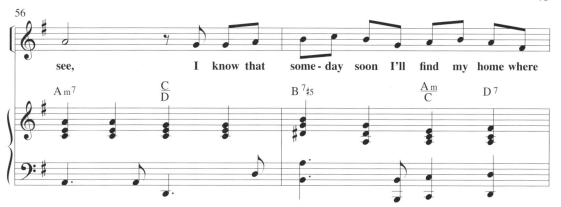

see, I know that some-day soon I'll find my home where

CD: 42

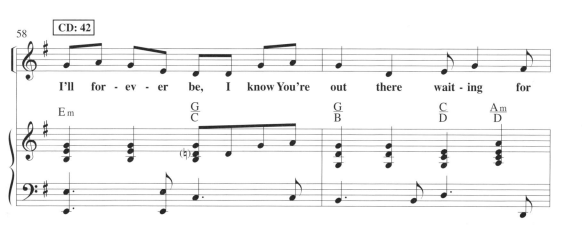

I'll for-ev-er be, I know You're out there wait-ing for

SHEPHERD BOY
mp

LEVI
mp

I know You're out there, I know You're

me.

out there, I know You're out there wait-ing for me.

Scene 6

GI JEFF *(wakes up the other toys)*: Rise and shine, soldiers! It's Christmas. Put that doll smile on your face.

HATCHBOX CAR: You're so right, GI Jeff. No matter what, we should celebrate Jesus' birth!

BABY DOLL: Listen everyone. Someone's coming.

HATCHBOX CAR: It's Mr. Goodman and Tommy.

SHINE BEAR: I thought the store was closed on Christmas.

GI JEFF: Get back to your places, on the double! Move it, toys! Move it!

BABY DOLL: Oh no, I'm getting nervous. And baby dolls should never get nervous!

SHINE BEAR: Hold on, Baby Doll.

GI JEFF: Attention, everyone! Freeze!

Toy Freeze Music

Music and Arr. by
JOHN DEVRIES

(The toys freeze. Smoke appears and the toys turn back into real toys on the shelves. This happens by the toy actors placing the pretend toys on the shelves and exiting quickly stage right and left to hide. MR. GOODMAN *and* TOMMY *enter the store.* MR. GOODMAN *carries a bag and places it on the counter.)*

MR. GOODMAN: I appreciate your coming in so early on Christmas. You know I wouldn't ask unless it was an emergency.

TOMMY: Sure thing, Mr. Goodman. What's up?

(While MR. GOODMAN *speaks,* TOMMY *is gathering the toys.)*

MR. GOODMAN: Our church is gathering food and toys for needy families. The ladies of the church have taken care of the food and you and I are going to take care of the toys. Come, Tommy, let's get started on this list.

TOMMY: But all these toys would be great in that After Christmas Sale.

MR. GOODMAN: I know, but giving these toys to those kids and knowing that they will be happy on Christmas will give <u>me</u> pure joy. Remember, the Joyland Toy Store's mission statement is, "We give toys in a spirit of joy." I can't think of a better way to spread the love of Jesus this Christmas, can you, Tommy?

TOMMY: I'm with you, boss.

MR. GOODMAN: Crank up that Christmas soundtrack. Turn up those Nativity lights. We've lots of toys to gather and no time to spare. Let's start with the Anderson children. What toys are on their list? We're on a mission, Tommy. Operation Merry Christmas!

(Music begins; during the song, TOMMY *and* MR. GOODMAN *gather up the toys for needy families. They leave* GI JEFF, HATCHBOX CAR, SHINE BEAR, *and* BABY DOLL *on the shelves.* MARY *and* JOSEPH *enter the manger scene to represent the nativity. This can be a living manger scene or an outdoor light up manger scene.)*

Carols of Fun

includes
The First Noel
Angels We Have Heard on High
Go, Tell It on the Mountain
We Wish You a Merry Christmas
O Come, Let Us Adore Him

Arr. by John DeVries

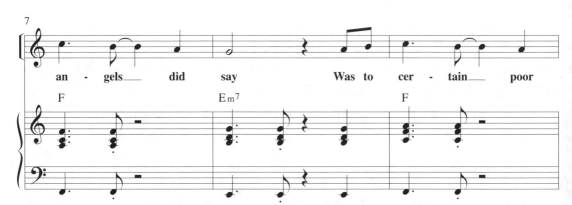

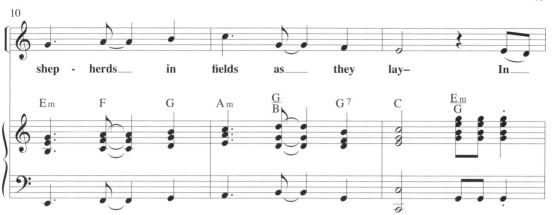

shep - herds___ in fields as___ they lay– In___

fields_____ where___ they lay___ keep - ing___ their

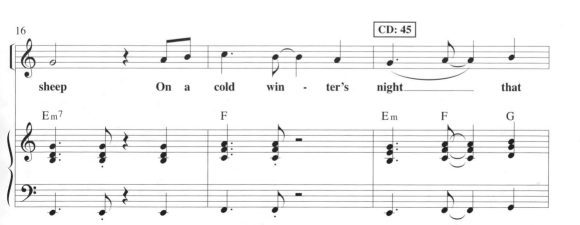

sheep On a cold win - ter's night_____ that

CD: 46

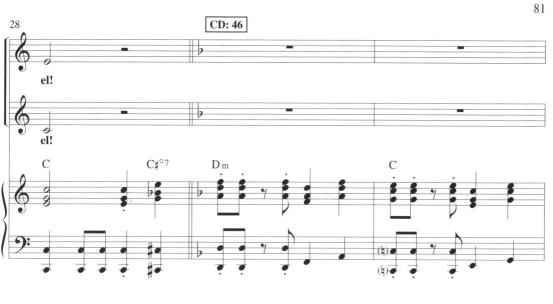

*"Angels We Have Heard on High"
ALL
mf

An - gels   we   have

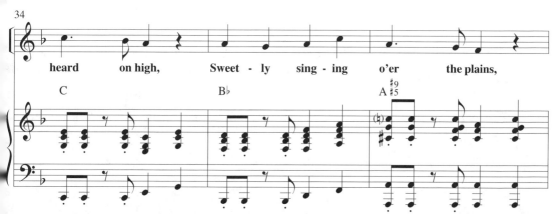

heard   on high,   Sweet - ly   sing - ing   o'er   the plains,

*"Go, Tell It on the Mountain"

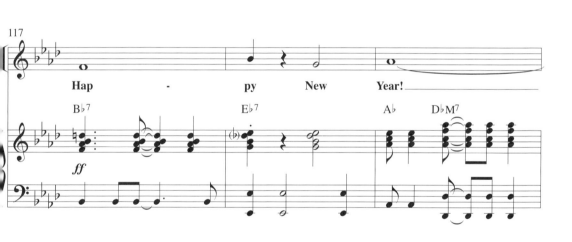

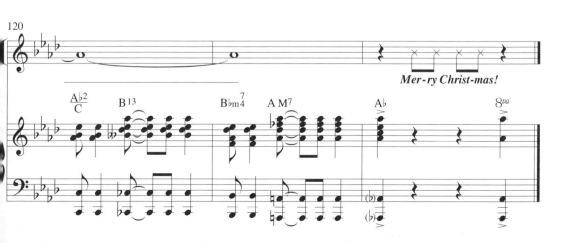

Scene 7

MR. GOODMAN: Whoo! *(wipes his forehead with a handkerchief)* Is that everyone, Tommy?

TOMMY: Williams was the last name on the list. I think that about does it, sir.

MR. GOODMAN: I have one more name to add…the Sanders family. Mr. Sanders died last year and they're having a really hard time. Get that box over there with the big turkey. Then, put GI Jeff, Hatchbox Car, Shine Bear, and Baby Doll in a bag.

TOMMY: Sure thing. *(goes and gets the toys and puts them in a bag)*

MR. GOODMAN: That leftover Shepherd Boy looks kind of lonely over there.

(TOMMY retrieves the shepherd and hands him to MR. GOODMAN)

MR. GOODMAN: Let's throw him in the bag. He's kind of like a lost sheep.

TOMMY: Right. Let's give him a home.

MR. GOODMAN: It might even remind the Sanders that even though they're feeling kind of lost without Mr. Sanders, that Jesus will take care of them. The love of Jesus is the best gift we can give anyone, Tommy.

TOMMY: Great, Mr. Goodman. You know, that name fits you, sir…you <u>are</u> a good man.

MR. GOODMAN: Thanks, Tommy. Let's be off. Oh, yes, and by the way Merry Christmas!

TOMMY: Merry Christmas to you, too, Mr. Goodman.

MR. GOODMAN: Let the giving begin!

(Music begins; during song, there are several examples of people giving to needy families. This could also be a power point experience.)

Give a Gift This Christmas

Words and Music by
PAM ANDREWS
Arr. by John DeVries

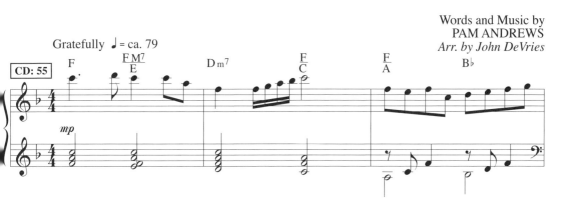

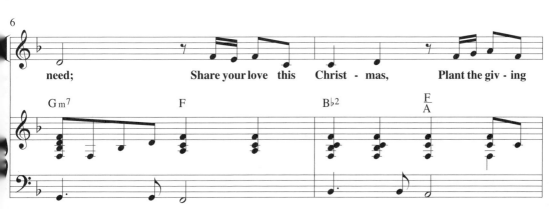

Scene 8

(MR. GOODMAN and TOMMY knock on the door. They leave the box of food and bag of toys then run away. MRS. SANDERS, LEVI, and CLARA enter from stage right into the living room scene.)

LEVI: Come on, Mom. I'm sure I heard something.

CLARA: I heard it, too, Mom. There was a noise outside!

MRS. SANDERS: Okay, kids. I'm sure it was nothing, but I'll have a look. *(sees the box of food)* Oh, my! Someone has left this big box of goodies on our porch.

CLARA *(excited)*: It's food!

LEVI *(excited)*: And a turkey! Thank You, Jesus! You're awesome!

MRS. SANDERS (*looks in the box*): Oh my! And there are potatoes, green beans, and lettuce for a salad. And look there's even the makings for Levi's favorite…pumpkin pie!

CLARA: Who would do this for us, mom?

MRS. SANDERS: Jesus gave us all this. Even though times have been hard, Jesus has always been there.

LEVI: That's so neat. Come on, Clara. Let's take this box to the kitchen.

(*There is another knock on the door. It is* MR. GOODMAN *and* TOMMY. MRS. SANDERS *goes to the door.*)

MRS. SANDERS: Hello, Mr. Goodman. Hello, Tommy.

MR. GOODMAN: Hello, Mrs. Sanders.

TOMMY: Merry Christmas!

MRS. SANDERS: Thank you for the box of food.

MR. GOODMAN: Just think of that food as gifts from heaven's table, Mrs. Sanders. In my haste, I forgot to leave this. Tommy and I were getting rid of some toys at the store…you know, cleaning house, and thought your kids might enjoy these. (*hands the bag to* MRS. SANDERS)

MRS. SANDERS: You're so kind, Mr. Goodman. You, too, Tommy. Thanks so much and Merry Christmas!

MR. GOODMAN: Merry Christmas to you, too!

(TOMMY *and* MR. GOODMAN *exit stage right.* LEVI *and* CLARA *run back into the room.*)

MRS. SANDERS: Look, kids. There was another bag…and I think it has your name on it.

(kids excitedly look in to the bag)

CLARA: Look, there's Baby Doll and Shine Bear. Mom, it lights up!

LEVI: And there's that Hatchbox Car I wanted and the GI Jeff. Cool! *(excited)* Look, it's the shepherd from the manger scene. It's a miracle! God heard my prayer! I knew He would! God sent him to us. *(puts the shepherd in the manger scene under the tree)* He's not alone now. He's with his family.

MRS. SANDERS: We're together, too, Levi. We're so blessed.

LEVI: This Christmas might not be so bad after all, mom. Thanks to Jesus.

CLARA: Merry Christmas, Mom.

MRS. SANDERS: Merry Christmas, kids. I love you.

(family freezes)

(music begins)

SPEAKER: Christmas is a wonderful time of year. Family and friends are all around. We decorate our Christmas Tree. We hang wreaths on the door. We buy presents for each other. This Christmas, let's make a real difference. Let's go beyond the glitz and glitter of the season to the real meaning of Christmas. Jesus came to earth to give. Let's give back to Jesus. One of the best ways we can do this is by giving to our neighbor. Jesus said, "I tell you the truth, whatever you did for one of the least of these brothers of mine, you did for Me." *(Matthew 25:40 NIV)* Give according to what you have, and as you give to others, Jesus will bless you. We hope you have a very Merry Christmas and have the joy of Jesus in your heart.

Underscore
(I Know You're Out There)

Words and Music by
PAM ANDREWS
Arr. by John DeVries

Joyland Finale

includes

Joyful, Joyful, We Adore Thee
Joy Down in My Heart
Joy to the World
Give a Gift This Christmas
Joyland Christmas

Driving ♩ = ca. 138

Arr. by John DeVries

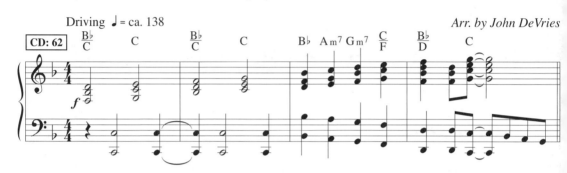

*"Joyful, Joyful, We Adore Thee"

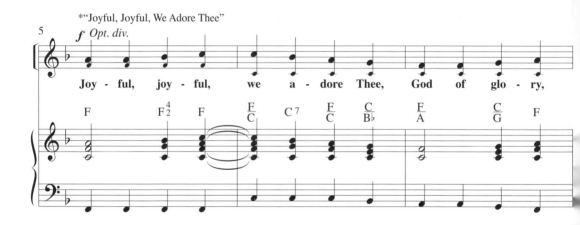

Joy - ful, joy - ful, we a - dore Thee, God of glo - ry,

Lord of love; Hearts un - fold like flow'rs be - fore Thee,

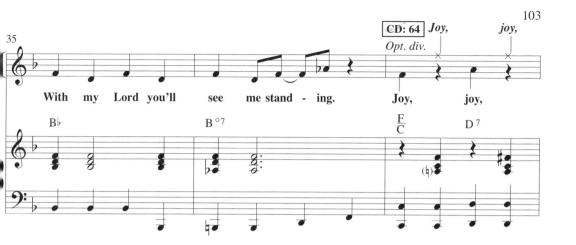

CD: 64

With my Lord you'll see me stand - ing. Joy, joy, Joy, joy,

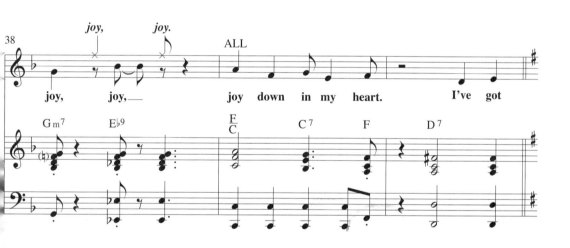

joy, joy,— joy down in my heart. I've got

I've got peace in my heart,— peace down in my heart.—

peace down in my heart this Christ - mas, peace down in my heart.

104

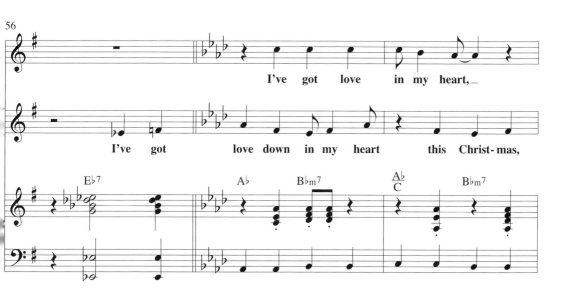

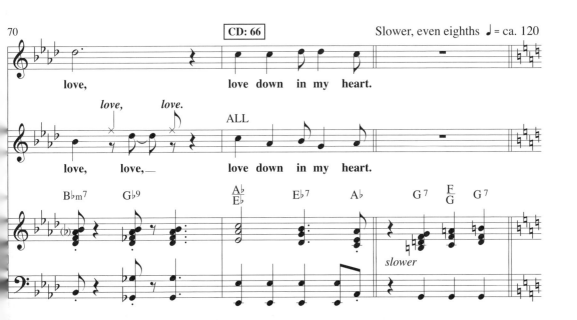

108   *"Joy to the World"

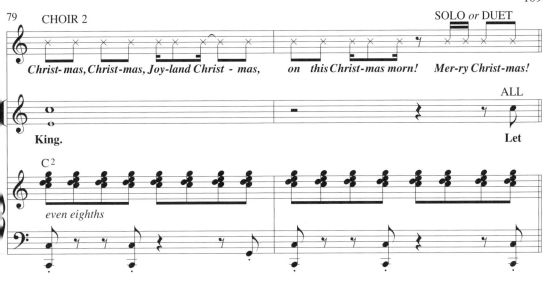

CHOIR 2 — SOLO or DUET

Christ-mas, Christ-mas, Joy-land Christ - mas, on this Christ-mas morn! Mer-ry Christ-mas!

King. / ALL / Let

C2 / even eighths

ev-'ry__ heart__ pre - pare__ Him__ room,__ And

C / Gm7 / C / Gm7 / C

heav'n and na - ture__ sing, And__ heav'n and na - ture__ sing, And__

C / A7 / Dm / G7

CD: 67

*"Give a Gift This Christmas"

SOLO *or* DUET

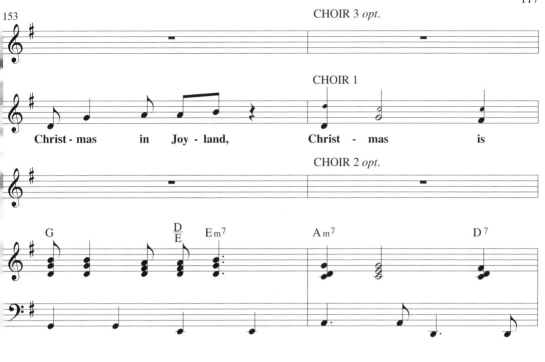

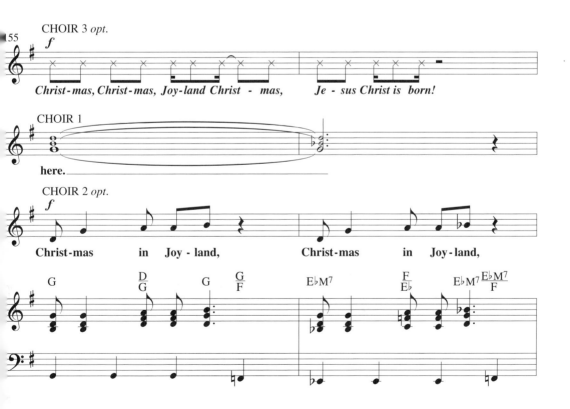

157

Christ - mas, Christ - mas, Joy - land Christ - mas, on this Christ - mas morn!

Christ - mas in Joy - land, Christ - mas is

Christ - mas in Joy - land, Christ - mas is

G D/G G D sus D

159

Je - sus Christ __ is, Je - sus Christ __ is born!

here! _____

here. _____

G G/F C/E Cm/Eb G/D G/B G 8va

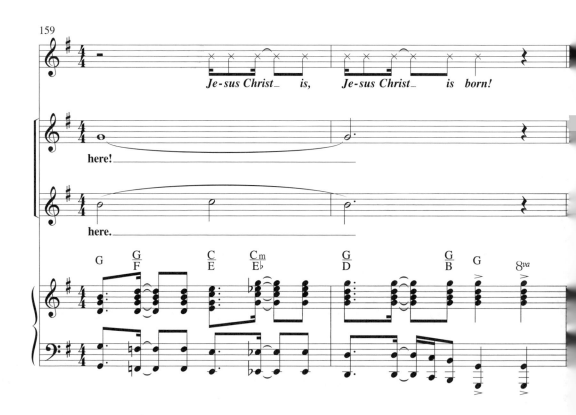

Joyland Curtain Call

includes
Joy Down in My Heart
Joyland Christmas

Gospel shuffle ♩ = ca. 180

Arr. by John DeVries

*"Joy Down in My Heart"

120

Slower, even eighths ♩ = ca. 120

52 CD: 74

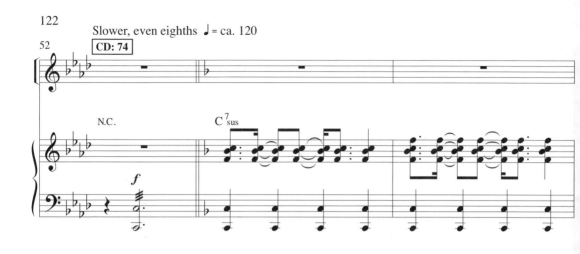

N.C.   C$^7_{sus}$

f

55

57 *"Joyland Christmas"   SOLO *or* DUET
                                                               mf

Mer-ry Christ-mas!

CHOIR *chant*
mf

Christ-mas, Christ-mas, Joy-land Christ - mas,   Je - sus Christ is born!

$\frac{F}{C}$ $\frac{Gm^7}{C}$

mf

124

Je - sus, we a - dore You, Sav - ior and our King; Je - sus, we a - dore You, our all, our ev - 'ry - thing; You make us want to sing!

CD: 78

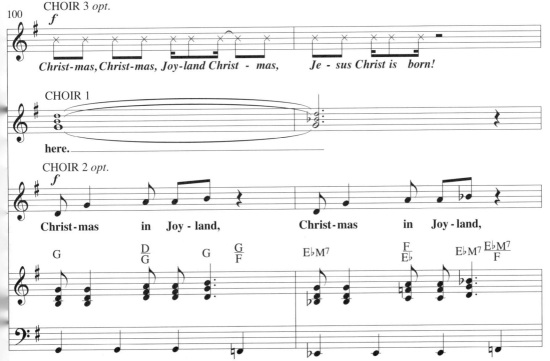

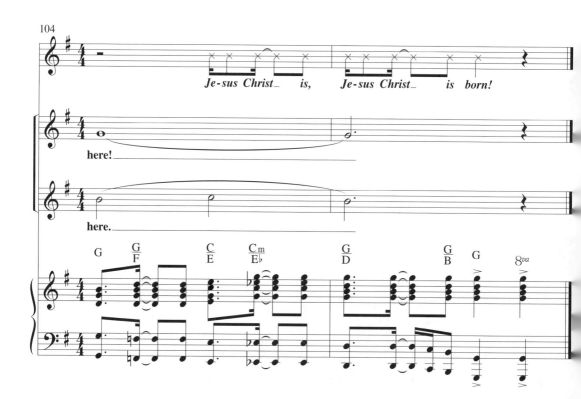

PRODUCTION NOTES

Setting

Joyland Toy Store set is center stage. The Sanders family living room scene is stage right. You could have a Christmas Tree, chair, lamp, end table, and rug. The manger scene should be stage left. There should only be a manger with a baby OR you could have a light-up manger scene like the ones we see in front of businesses at Christmas. The choir should be center stage. There is a backdrop design provided for you in the "Joyland" Resource Notebook and complete construction ideas on the "Joyland" Video.

Casting Ideas

Do you have a large, middle-sized, or small choir? Don't worry, this musical is perfect for any size choir. You may do the musical as written utilizing only the main characters if you have a smaller choir. If your choir is large, you may want to divide parts or add solos. Be creative. Give everyone a part if possible. Giving every child some kind of special part will encourage attendance and participation. Pray and God will lead you to the right decisions.

Cast

Mrs. Sanders   _____

Clara Sanders   _____

Levi Sanders   _____

Mr. Goodman   _____

Tommy   _____

Specialty Movement

To move or not to move?
In an effort to supply the needs of all our churches, we are providing you with choreography for this children's choir musical. We realize that according to various denominations, this might or might not be appropriate for your church. We encourage you to seek the leadership of your church and seek the Lord in prayer as you make your decision. God bless YOU and know we are always here for questions or comments.

Note: The movement is found in the "Joyland" Resource Notebook or on the "Joyland" Video.

"Joyland" Movement Team

_____

_____

_____

_____

Cast and Costume

Cast

Mrs. Sanders - This part can be played by an adult or child. She should wear a mother type outfit. She might want to add a Christmas sweater. It should be obvious that she is not well to do. She should wear a robe, house shoes, and pajamas in the home scene.

Clara Sanders - She should wear a kid Christmas outfit. She could wear a Christmas sweat shirt and jeans. It should be obvious that she is not well to do. She should wear a robe, house shoes, and pajamas in the home scene.

Levi Sanders - He should wear what any normal boy would wear, a sweat shirt and jeans would be fine. It should be obvious that he is not well to do. He should wear a robe, house shoes, and pajamas in the home scene.

Mr. Goodman - This part can be played by an adult or child. He should wear khaki colored pants, a white shirt, and store apron.

Tommy - He should wear jeans, a white shirt, and store apron.

Toys

Note: Find toys in a local toy store similar to these characters. Match the costuming to the toys.

GI Jeff - He should wear a camo outfit and helmet and should look like an army man. Try to avoid using gun accessories. You will also need a toy version of this character.

Baby Doll - She should look like any baby doll. You may want a fluffy skirt and hair bow. You may want a sleeper style baby doll. She might have a large pacifier which can be purchased at a costume shop. You will also need a toy version of this character.

Hatchbox Car - He should look like a car with a driver. Put the child in a race car driver style jacket and jeans and hang a box made to look like a car around his neck. You will also need a toy version of this character.

Shine Bear - He/She should look like a bear that lights up. You should make him/her a bear costume with a jumpsuit cover. This costume should have a cordless punch-on light made into the belly of the bear jump suit costume so at one point, Shine Bear can light up. You will also need a toy version of this character. You can do the same to the toy bear. Just add a jump suit and small punch-on light.

Shepherd Boy - He should be dressed in a regular shepherd boy costume from your church's costume closet. You will also need a toy version of this character.

Choir - The speaking parts should wear the Joyland T-Shirt and jeans.

To purchase these T-shirts, contact:

> Personalized Gifts & Apparel
> Tom Roland, Owner
> (800) 898-6170
> (615) 822-3452
> Website: www.pg4u.com
> Email: info@pg4u.com

OR you can download the T-shirt art from the Lillenas website at www.lillenas.com to create your own shirt.

Specialty Movement Team

The Specialty Movement Team costuming is found in the "Joyland" Resource Notebook.

Set Design

The following is the layout of the set:

Toy Store Backdrop

Risers

Toy Store shelves   Toy Store Shelves
                                          Check out

Sanders Home   Outside Nativity

soloists   soloists
X X   X X

Props

GI Jeff Toy Version	Baby Doll Toy Version
Hatchbox Car Toy Version	Shine Bear Toy Version
Shepherd Boy Toy Version	Other toys
Store shelves	Cash register
Check-out table	Check-out sign
Feather duster	Broom
Ninja Nedi	Purse
Money: small change	Watch
Glass of water	Christmas Tree
Nativity Set	Outdoor Manger Scene (living or pretend)
Batteries	Food boxes
Toy bags	Pretend turkey

Food Items: especially potatoes, green beans, lettuce, canned pumpkin pie

Solos

Overture	No Solos
Joyland Christmas	No Solos Small Group Harmony
Let Us Bring Joy to You	GI Jeff Solo Baby Doll Solo Hatchbox Car Solo Shine Bear Solo Small Group Harmony
God's Got a Plan for Me	Shepherd Boy Solo Small Group Harmony
What Child Is This?	Mrs. Sanders Solo Small Group Harmony
Shine Your Light for Jesus	Shine Bear Solo Small Group Harmony
I Know You're Out There	Levi Shepherd Boy
Carols of Fun	No Solos Small Group Harmony
Give a Gift This Christmas	Solo Verse 1 Solo Verse 2
Joyland Finale	Solo (Joy Down in My Heart) Small Group Harmony
Joyland Curtain Call	No Solos

Microphone Needs

It would be good to have a cordless lavaliere microphone for each main character. Hand-held microphones can be used as a substitute. Place two solo microphones on stands stage left and stage right to accommodate the solos.

Scripture References

Overture - Psalm 28:7 NIV
> The LORD is my strength and my shield; my heart trusts in Him, and I am helped. My heart leaps for joy and I will give thanks to Him in song.

Joyland Christmas - Isaiah 9:6 NIV
> For to us a Child is born, to us a Son is given, and the government will be on His shoulders. And He will be called Wonderful Counselor, Mighty God, Everlasting Father, Prince of Peace.

Let Us Bring Joy to You - Psalms 5:11 NIV
> But let all who take refuge in You be glad; let them ever sing for joy. Spread Your protection over them, that those who love Your name may rejoice in You.

God's Got a Plan for Me - Proverbs 3:5-6 NIV
> Trust in the LORD with all your heart and lean not on your own understanding; in all your ways acknowledge Him, and He will make your paths straight.

What Child Is This? - Luke 2:10-11 NIV
> But the angel said to them, "Do not be afraid. I bring you good news of great joy that will be for all the people. Today in the town of David a Savior has been born to you; He is Christ the Lord."

Shine Your Light for Jesus - Psalm 19:8 NIV
> The precepts of the LORD are right, giving joy to the heart. The commands of the LORD are radiant, giving light to the eyes.

I Know You're Out There - Psalm 121:1-2 NIV
> I lift up my eyes to the hills– where does my help come from? My help comes from the LORD, the maker of heaven and earth.

Carols of Fun - Micah 5:2 NIV
> But you, Bethlehem…out of you will come for me one who will be ruler over Israel, whose origins are from of old, from ancient times.

Give a Gift This Christmas - Matthew 25:40 NIV
> The King will reply, 'I tell you the truth, whatever you did for one of the least of these brothers of mine, you did for Me.'"

Joyland Finale - Galatians 5:22-23 NIV
> But the fruit of the Spirit is love, joy, peace, patience, kindness, goodness, faithfulness, gentleness and self-control. Against such things there is no law.

Joyland Curtain Call - Nehemiah 8:10 NIV
> Go and enjoy choice food and sweet drinks, and send some to those who have nothing prepared. This day is sacred to our Lord. Do not grieve, for the joy of the LORD is your strength.